> 66 **The Church of England is at serious risk of doing some joined-up thinking.** 99

With these words in 2004, the First Church Estates Commissioner, Andreas Whittam Smith, welcomed both *Mission-shaped Church* and the proposals that have given birth to Bishops' Mission Orders. The two were always meant to go together, as imagination in the Church is released and then focused.

This joined-up thinking continues. We now have a piece of legislation, the **Dioceses, Pastoral and Mission Measure 2007**, which has been warmly approved by the General Synod and accepted by Parliament. Within it we have the section on **Bishops' Mission Orders (BMOs)**, and the House of Bishops' **Code of Practice** on how to make that section work in the dioceses. This Code, in its turn, was approved by the General Synod in early 2008. It's legal. All we have to do now is use it.

Using the law is a painstaking, complex and measured business, as you will see as you read this booklet. But it is worth the effort. Because all over the country, we now have fresh expressions of church that should be able to take their place within their dioceses, as valued and legally constituted partners with the established parishes around them.

Bishops' Mission Orders are not imposed without reference to others. They are collaborative by nature. They are made by bishops so that pioneers can do their work. By making an Order, the bishop endorses and authorizes the project that it covers, and therefore needs to be satisfied that it is the right way forward. Orders are made after serious consultation with those who have an interest in, or are affected by, what the Orders are intending to do.

In short, BMOs bring what Archbishop Rowan has called 'a careful and principled loosening of the structures'. They are a tool to enable the mission of God. They are there so that things can *happen*. This seems biblical enough – and Anglican enough. St Paul rightly said (1 Corinthians 14.40) that all things should be done decently and in order – but he did say that all things should be done!

The Measure refers to mission initiatives that would be likely to promote or further the Church's mission 'through fostering or developing a form of Christian community'. These new communities may take many forms, including some that are relatively traditional in outlook, but many are likely to be 'fresh expressions of church'. That is why the Code of Practice uses the new term, and why this guide uses it as a general term to cover communities of the kind referred to in the Measure. The working definition of a fresh expression of church is as follows.

Fresh expressions

A fresh expression is a form of church for our changing culture established primarily for the benefit of people who are not yet members of any church.

- It will come into being through principles of listening, service, incarnational mission and making disciples.

- It will have the potential to become a mature expression of church shaped by the gospel and the enduring marks of the church and for its cultural context.

Is it always necessary to have a Bishop's Mission Order?

Not always. There are lots of ways to engage in God's mission. For example, you don't need a Bishop's Mission Order for a traditional parish mission, for a one-off special event, or for a new way of serving the community.

You don't need a BMO to begin a fresh expression of church that is integral to a single parish's ministry (for example, a youth congregation or a new Saturday evening service). Support for this kind of venture comes through the normal parish structures. The same may well apply where parishes are collaborating within a single benefice.

Having said that, if a fresh expression of church grows and develops within a single parish or benefice, it may be right to consider a BMO as part of its journey to maturity.

Possible examples are as follows:

- A new congregation meeting in a school may need to grow up and take its place in the life of the deanery.

- A youth congregation may be 'owned' and developed by a number of churches who share in supporting a youth pastor.

- A network of cells that forms a church across a benefice may need to be recognized as part of the overall governance of the benefice.

Bishops' Mission Orders

a beginner's guide

THE CHURCH
OF ENGLAND

Bishops' Mission Orders
a beginner's guide

This booklet is a simple guide for clergy, PCCs and deanery synods to a vital new piece of Church of England legislation: the **Bishop's Mission Order**.

In 2004, the General Synod commended the report *Mission-shaped Church: Church planting and fresh expressions of church in a changing context*. We are now engaging at every level with encouraging fresh expressions of church in parishes, deaneries, dioceses and nationally. Many of these fresh expressions can – and do – flourish and grow within the traditional parish structure. But often they are collaborative ventures between or across parish boundaries. Often they involve collaboration with other churches. This is the type of case where a Bishop's Mission Order may be what is needed. Potentially, Bishops' Mission Orders may affect every parish and deanery in the land over the next ten years.

Fresh expressions of church are developing alongside and within the parish system as part of a growing mixed economy of church life. All churches of whatever kind are called to engage in God's mission to the whole of God's world. All churches are called to work together constructively in serving that common purpose.

Every PCC and deanery synod, therefore, needs to come to grips with the opportunities. This involves understanding what is now possible within the new legislation and why it is necessary. If you are actively involved in seeking a Bishop's Mission Order, then you will need to refer at every stage to the House of Bishops' Code of Practice as well as to this booklet. There is a list of other resources and agencies on pages 14–15. Even where a fresh expression of church or some other new venture does not need a Bishop's Mission Order, the Code may well be a helpful source of guidance and creative ideas.

We hope and pray that, as the Church of England begins to work with this new framework, there will be creativity and a new fruitfulness in mission that will be of long-lasting benefit to the whole of the society we serve.

Paul Bayes and Steven Croft

An Order may well be helpful and necessary when:

- Your mission initiative aims to establish a new community (a fresh expression of church); and
- A number of parishes or ecumenical partners are involved.

In summary, the Bishop's Mission Order provisions are intended for situations where the bishop is satisfied that the initiative would be likely to promote or further the mission of the Church through fostering or developing a distinctive Christian community which will itself be part of the wider Church of England. **Code of Practice 1.12.13**

Possible examples include:

- A new network congregation for young adults across a town or city;
- Revitalization of an existing congregation in a socially and economically deprived part of a city, built on structured partnership between two or more parishes and the drawing-in of new resources;
- The ecumenical appointment of a schools' worker to three local secondary schools with the intention of creating a Christian community;
- A congregation that primarily serves the needs of a particular ethnic group seeks formal affiliation with the Church of England;
- Collaborative work between three parishes and the Methodist Circuit to plant a missional Christian community in an area of new housing development.

If you are not certain whether the venture you have in mind would need an Order, your bishop will advise you on whom to consult in the first instance.

Stages in the process

There are three stages to the process of granting an Order:

Stage 1
Making the proposal
and
Initial explorations

Stage 2
Consultation
and
Drafting the order

Stage 3
Making the order
and
Review

If the fresh expression is **starting from scratch**, this process may take several months. The work of developing the proposals for the fresh expression should normally continue during the process of seeking a Bishop's Mission Order.

If the fresh expression is **already in existence**, it will normally be possible to move early parts of the process along more rapidly.

Stages in the process

Stage 1

Making the proposal
and
Initial explorations

Stage 2

Consultation
and
Drafting the order

Stage 3

Making the order
and
Review

STAGE 1:
Making the proposal *and* Initial explorations

Making the proposal

It may sound obvious, but Bishops' Mission Orders are made by bishops, acting as leaders in God's mission in their dioceses. In making an Order, the bishop endorses and authorizes the initiative that the Order covers. The bishop therefore needs to be satisfied that the proposal will contribute properly to the mission of God in the diocese.

An Order may come about in one of two ways:

- Those who have what the Measure calls 'ecclesiastical functions' in the diocese may make a formal request to the bishop for one. This may mean a single individual, or a group or body of people – an incumbent or incumbents, a PCC, a deanery synod, a Church Army evangelist or any combination. The request can come from someone other than the people who wish to put the proposal into action. A formal request of this kind will then receive proper consideration by the bishop.

- Alternatively, the bishop may decide to make an Order in a particular case even without receiving a formal request. It may spring from the bishop's own initiative, or from informal suggestions or proposals made by anyone concerned. The bishop can then decide whether it would be worth considering the idea of a Bishop's Mission Order as the best way of taking matters forward.

So a good way to begin is to have an initial conversation exploring your ideas with the bishop or bishop's officer. Then, when you are ready to make a definite proposal, you should write to the bishop to begin the formal process. Your letter should answer the following questions:

1. What is the nature and scope of the proposal?
2. Who are the originating parties?
3. How will the proposal further the mission of the Church?
4. Are ecumenical partners involved at this stage or envisaged?
5. Why is a Bishop's Mission Order required?

6

Initial explorations

Once the bishop has received a formal request or decided some other proposal should be considered, the process of initial exploration will begin. The bishop will normally delegate this task to a 'bishop's officer' who may be an archdeacon, missioner or other person. The officer should not be closely involved in the proposals or affected by them.

> The scope and extent of the initial explorations will to some extent be dependent on the nature of the project. In the case of a well-developed project that has been established for some years, it may be possible to proceed directly to the next stage of the process. **Code of Practice 2.4.3**

Consultations at this stage

The initial explorations will normally involve a meeting with the group who have made the proposal or who are most closely involved in the project.

There will also be preliminary consultations with all those who are not directly involved in the proposal but are likely to be most affected by the BMO (for example, the incumbents or priests in charge of any parishes involved). These may be written consultations or face-to-face meetings. The bishop's staff meeting and the Diocesan Mission and Pastoral Committee will also have the opportunity to comment. The bishop or the bishop's officer may also decide that other consultations would be helpful in the particular case.

From these initial consultations, the bishop's officer will write a report building on the proposal. That report will normally give more detailed answers to Questions 1 to 5. It will also seek to answer Questions 6 to 12 shown on the right.

The finished report will be sent to those making the original proposal and the bishop. The bishop now has enough information to decide whether or not to move forward and proceed to Stage 2. This decision is the bishop's alone. If the bishop decides not to proceed, the reasons will be explained to anyone who submitted a formal request for an Order.

6 How will what is proposed complement existing mission initiatives?

7 What resources are needed to begin and sustain the project? Have Anglican and ecumenical partnerships been considered? Are there others who might be able to contribute?

8 What parties may need to be consulted formally as part of the process of the granting of a Bishop's Mission Order?

9 Is appropriate mission accompaniment in place or envisaged for the venture?

10 What steps will be made in the Order for the provision of ministry? This should include exploring provision for the sacraments of Baptism and the Eucharist at the point at which this becomes appropriate.

11 What thought has been given to the long-term future and sustainability of the venture? (Note that this does not rule out projects that are always intended to be medium-term in nature.)

12 Are there any special circumstances that will need to be explored further in the formal consideration of the Order?

You will find a more detailed version of these questions in the Code at **2.4.7**.

Stages in the process

Stage 1
Making the proposal
and
Initial explorations

Stage 2
Consultation
and
Drafting the order

Stage 3
Making the order
and
Review

STAGE 2:
Consultation *and* Drafting the order

Drafting the order

If the bishop decides it is right to proceed to the next stage, then the registrar of the diocese will normally be asked to draw up an initial draft of a Bishop's Mission Order, which can be used in the formal consultation.

A BMO is meant to give flexible, light-touch authorization. Every Order will be different. Registrars will have sample orders and skeleton documents, and details of where these are available from will also be provided on the Share website (see p. 15).

The draft Order must specify:

- what the mission initiative is – and normally what it is (or will be) called;
- what the initiative's objectives are;
- where the initiative is being (or is to be) carried out;
- who will lead the initiative and be responsible to the bishop for it, and normally how they are appointed and replaced;
- the role of the leader(s);
- what needs to be done for the administration of the sacraments;
- who the Visitor for the initiative will be (see page 10);
- what the duration of the Order is (a maximum of five years in the first instance).

The Order may also:

- Authorize the initiative's ministers to exercise their ministry in a specified place and in any specified manner. It may also authorize them to do so without the permission of the minister who has the cure of souls there (see p. 9);
- Authorize public worship in any building (other than a church), with the consent of the person who has the general management and control of the building;
- Authorize public worship in any church building, with the consent of any minister having the cure of souls there.

See section **5.1** of the Code for more details.

The Code also lists some other areas that can be dealt with, either in the Order or in an additional Supplementary Instrument. These would normally include:

- The terms and conditions of service of any licensed ministers or others with a role in the initiative, and the process for replacing them where necessary (the minister's licence will be separate from the Order itself);

- The organization, governance and financing of the initiative, including the management and control of property;

- Any measures required for the protection of children, young persons and other vulnerable people, and for health and safety and insurance;

- Relationships between persons involved with the mission initiative and those who have the cure of souls in any area to which the Order relates, and with other churches;

- Possible representation on the deanery synod or synods.

You will find additional full notes covering all of these areas, and the practical arrangements for governance and accounting, in the Code of Practice and other resources referred to on Share (see p. 15).

Consultation

The Code details (**2.5.4**) the nature and principles that should underlie consultation. These include the principle of fairness to all, consulting before decisions have been taken and giving adequate time for response, and providing those who are consulted with sufficient information about the proposals and the reasons for them, so that they can respond effectively. This means that a first draft of the Order will normally form at least part of the basis of the consultation.

Ministry without the consent of the minister who has cure of souls

The Measure permits the bishop to include in the Order, after special statutory consultation, a provision authorizing a minister to exercise his or her ministry in a place, for the purpose of the initiative or in connection with it, *without* the consent of the person who has the cure of souls there. Particular consultation is needed under the Measure before this can happen. This provision is intended:

1 For situations where the present incumbent or priest in charge consents but the mission initiative needs the security of being able to continue;

2 For cases where the initiative will cover a large geographical area, where having to identify all the individual incumbents who would otherwise need to consent and obtain their agreement would be impracticable or place real problems in the way of the initiative achieving its objectives;

3 For cases where the present incumbent or priest in charge is unwilling to give such consent, and the bishop, after consultation, is satisfied that it is right to override this.

In all cases the bishop will need to consult:

- those who have a significant interest in, or will be affected by, the initiative;
- leaders of other churches;
- the Diocesan Mission and Pastoral Committee.

However, the bishop also has to decide whether it would also be right to consult anyone else in the particular case.

If a formal partnership with other churches is involved, the bishop will also consult representatives of the other denominations. There is detailed information in the Code to help you navigate through sometimes complex ecumenical guidelines, and further advice can be obtained from the diocesan ecumenical adviser.

If there is to be provision to exercise ministry in a particular place without the consent of the minister with the cure of souls, then the bishop must also consult the incumbents affected, either individually (for a small area) or through the deanery or diocesan House of Clergy. (See section **4.4.9** of the Code for full details.) The bishop should do this by writing to those who need to be consulted, with all the necessary information.

Stages in the process

Stage 1

Making the proposal
and
Initial explorations

Stage 2

Consultation
and
Drafting the order

Stage 3

Making the order
and
Review

STAGE 3:
Making the order *and* Review

After the process of formal consultation, the bishop considers all the responses and decides whether or not to proceed with the Order. If the Order is to go forward, the bishop also decides whether any changes are needed to the draft of the Order used at the consultation stage.

The final draft of the Order is now prepared, together with a Supplementary Instrument if there is to be one. At this stage, the leaders of the initiative need to give their formal consent. Once this has happened, the bishop and the leaders sign the Order, and it comes into effect.

The role of the bishop's Visitor

See the Code of Practice sections **3.3** and **5.3**.

Hopefully, the vision of the fresh expression has been developing through the whole of this process. When the Order is in force, the role of the Visitor becomes vital to the initiative.

The Visitor is appointed by the bishop to give additional support and oversight to the initiative and its leaders. He or she will be an experienced priest or lay person appointed with the agreement of the initiative's leadership team. The bishop will probably establish a team of Visitors to BMO initiatives in the diocese. As with the bishop's officer, the Visitor cannot be someone already closely involved in the life of the initiative.

The leaders of the initiative have a duty:

- To consult the Visitor regularly about the general direction and development of the initiative;
- To supply the Visitor with copies of the annual accounts and any other information the Visitor needs to carry out his or her functions.

Visitors provide a key element in the structures of support, advice and encouragement, alongside coaching or mission accompaniment. Accompaniment gives each initiative one or more 'critical friends', who can support and challenge the leadership as things develop and new opportunities and problems come along. It is the Visitor's job to ensure that such accompaniment is in place. A number of agencies have been developing tools for mission accompaniment; you will find details of some of these among the resources on pages 14–15.

The Visitor is expected to have substantial contact with the initiative and its leaders at least twice a year and to report regularly in writing to the bishop (with copies sent to the leaders) with a fuller report at least every 18 months. The Visitor will also advise the bishop on the financial probity of the project and will give advice on appropriate structures for governing it. At the same time, if anyone else wishes to draw attention to anything regarding the initiative, they can bring it to the Visitor's notice.

Finally, as the period of the Order nears its end, the Visitor will lead a formal review (see right).

Reviewing the Order

A Bishop's Mission Order is made initially for up to five years. During this initial period, there will be a regular review of the initiative by the Visitor at least every 18 months.

Guidelines for this regular review are in the Code of Practice (at **6.1**). It is intended as a light-touch exercise, to help the initiative develop and fulfil its objectives. Dioceses are asked to develop their own material to guide reviews, and some suggested drafts are available on Share.

Towards the end of the initial period of up to five years, there will be a more formal review of the initiative, again led by the Visitor. This review will look back over the period, but will also assess how the initiative is developing and whether it continues to fulfil the original objectives. The review will also identify and consider options for the future.

At this point, there will again be formal consultation with the Diocesan Mission and Pastoral Committee, with any ecumenical partners and with other key parties interested in, or affected by, the initiative.

The Visitor's review

The Visitor's report will contain recommendations on:

- Whether the initiative should continue;
- Whether the Bishop's Mission Order should be renewed for a further five years or whether it should continue on some other basis – for example, whether some other legal provision can be made;
- Whether there should be any changes to the original Order;
- Any other formal recommendations or comments that the Visitor thinks important or that the bishop requests.

After a further period of up to five years, the initiative is reviewed again. If the bishop is satisfied that the initiative should continue and that there is no other suitable way of achieving that, then the Order can be renewed for an indefinite period.

Approaching the process

As we have seen, exploring authorization and endorsement for a fresh expression through a Bishop's Mission Order is a supportive process, but a demanding one. How should you approach it? It could be seen by some as an inconvenience or distraction from the work of mission. Or it can be seen as a godly, helpful way to sharpen and develop our involvement in the mission of God. Here are some reflections on the benefits of this process.

Testing a call

Before making any major decision, individuals are encouraged to test a sense of calling and count the cost of what they are about to do. That testing and discernment is also needed by communities. The process is designed to help you to reflect prayerfully on what you feel called to do by sharing it with others. As part of that process, you may decide not to proceed or to do things very differently. If you do go ahead, your commitment will be stronger.

Owning the vision

The Church is one body – the Body of Christ. It is essential that the different parts of the body know and value each other and support one another as we seek to work together for God's kingdom. The process of seeking a Bishop's Mission Order gives a framework for sharing information and vision about the initiative with a much wider group, inviting their support and prayer. It also gives a framework within which the bishop, advised by others in the diocese, can balance the different possibilities of moving forward within God's mission.

Securing continuity

Many ventures in mission never survive beyond the first, founding group. Enthusiasm wanes or key individuals move on, and what begins in a promising way is not sustained. Or a venture can grow and develop in a way that no one foresaw at the outset. A Bishop's Mission Order aims to hold the initiative within a much wider framework as a venture owned and supported by the whole diocese. There is a much greater chance then of continuity, growth and development over a long period of time.

Providing accountability

Exercising ministry in the Christian community is a serious responsibility, and all ministers are called to give account for what they are doing. A Bishop's Mission Order gives a framework of accountability and support to the bishop through the Visitor. The same framework ensures appropriate quality in Christian teaching and practice, compliance with legal and financial obligations, and protection of the vulnerable.

Getting there ...

The whole Church of England will be learning together over the next five years about how best to work with Bishops' Mission Orders to support strong and sustainable fresh expressions of church. We're feeling our way. Patience will be needed.

There is lots more good material in the Code of Practice that we haven't been able to summarize here, on (for example):

- Working together ecumenically;
- Worship in fresh expressions of church;
- Good systems for report and review;
- Developing ministry in fresh expressions of church.

You will find material to support this booklet (such as sample forms and orders) and lots of other emerging wisdom for fresh expressions of church on Share (see p. 15).

FAQs (eventually!)

As dioceses begin to develop Orders, we expect to see some frequently asked questions (FAQs). Unfortunately, we don't yet know what these will be! But as we begin to learn what they are, these FAQs (with some answers) will be posted on Share and on the Church of England website.

Help is at hand!

Pioneers are not alone. There are people in every diocese who would be delighted to help your church, or your initiative, work through the process of seeking a BMO. They include your bishops, archdeacons and diocesan missioners. The national Fresh Expressions team and Mission and Public Affairs division and other relevant staff of the Archbishops' Council are there to help, as are other mission agencies such as the Church Army, CMS and CPAS.

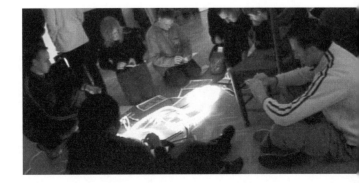

Where to get further help – a selection from the available material

The full text of the **Dioceses, Pastoral and Mission Measure 2007** is available at **www.opsi.gov.uk/uk-church-measures/cm-2007-index.htm**

The full text of the **Code of Practice** is available at **www.cofe.anglican.org\about\churchcommissioners\pastoral\bmocode** It includes the full text of the part of the Measure dealing with Bishops' Mission Orders.

As skeleton Orders and other resources are developed, they will appear on **www.sharetheguide.org** – a new resource created by Fresh Expressions and the Church Army in order to develop practical wisdom on planting and sustaining fresh expressions of church.

The Share website will also hold a developing list of **Frequently Asked Questions**, which will complement this booklet.

Books

Mission-shaped Church: Church planting and fresh expressions of church in a changing context, Graham Cray *et al.*, CHP, 2004

The foundational report for missional thinking around new mission initiatives/fresh expressions. See especially the chapter 'An Enabling Framework'.

The Future of the Parish System, Steven Croft (ed.), CHP, 2006

This includes articles on the theological undergirding of the mixed-economy church by Rowan Williams and Graham Cray and on developing good practice by Michael Moynagh.

Mission-shaped Questions, Steven Croft (ed.), CHP, 2008

Includes a summary of Church of England and Methodist developments since Mission-shaped Church, *as well as articles by 14 theologians on the ecclesiology and mission questions around fresh expressions of church, with pieces by Angela Tilby, John Hull, James Dunn and Lindsay Urwin among others.*

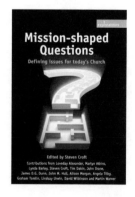

See also:

- **Resourcing Renewal: Shaping churches for the emerging future**, Martyn Atkins, Inspire, 2007

- **The Human Face of the Church: A social psychology and pastoral theology resource for pioneer and traditional ministry**, Sarah Savage and Eolene Boyd-Macmillan, Canterbury Press, 2007

- **Exiles: Living missionally in a post-Christian culture**, Michael Frost, Hendrickson, 2006

- **Gone for Good? A study in church leaving**, Leslie Francis and Philip Richter, Methodist Publishing House, 2008

- **The Road to Growth: Towards a thriving church**, Bob Jackson, CHP, 2006

- **Encounters on the Edge** (booklet series), George Lings, Church Army Sheffield Centre.

Booklets (sold in packs of 5) and all published by CHP:

- **Moving on in a Mission-shaped Church**, Steven Croft and George Lings, 2005

- **Starting a Fresh Expression**, Steven Croft, George Lings and Claire Dalpra, 2006

- **Listening for Mission**, Steven Croft, Freddy Hedley and Bob Hopkins, 2007

DVDs

Expressions: the DVD 1 – Stories of Church for a Changing World, produced and directed by Norman Ivison, CHP, 2005

Expressions: the DVD 2 – Changing Church in Every Place, produced and directed by Norman Ivison, CHP, 2006

Websites

www.freshexpressions.org.uk for news and stories from the Fresh Expressons initiative.

www.sharetheguide.org for developing practical wisdom on planting and sustaining fresh expressions of church.

www.encountersontheedge.org for access to Church Army's expertise and in-depth stories of new communities.

www.geocities.com/ccom_ctbi/Building_Bridges_of_Hope.html for details of the ecumenical 'Building bridges of hope' process from Churches Together in Britain and Ireland – one form of mission accompaniment.

66 The new legal provisions for Bishops' Mission Orders are intended to foster and support a range of new mission initiatives in ways not provided for in previous legislation. The provisions are based on principles of creativity, courtesy and collaboration, undergirding and supporting God's mission and the development of a mixed-economy church. This little booklet now provides clear and accessible advice on how to set about using this new legislation and its associated Code of Practice. I welcome and commend it as a practical tool for use by clergy, PCCs, deaneries, mission groups and others who are wanting to explore new terrain for the sake of the growth of the Church and the sharing of the Good News of Jesus Christ. 99

Michael Langrish,
Bishop of Exeter

Bishops' Mission Orders
a beginner's guide

Every PCC and deanery synod in the land needs to come to grips with the opportunities created by the new Bishops' Mission Orders. This simple booklet sets out when an Order may be needed, what it can and cannot do, and how the process will work.

In clear, accessible language, the booklet covers the background to the *Dioceses, Pastoral and Mission Measure 2007*, the consultation needed, the steps you need to follow, the role of the Visitor, drawing up an order and provision for review. This short guide is an essential starting point in making the most of a key piece of new legislation to support fresh expressions of church.

Copyright © Archbishops' Council 2008

Design and typesetting:
Hugh Hillyard-Parker, Edinburgh

Photographs:
Norman Ivison © Fresh Expressions

fresh expressions

CHURCH HOUSE
PUBLISHING

£6.00 (pack of 5)

ISBN 978-0-7151-4169-4

9 780715 141694 >